THE SCIENCE OF
NATURAL DISASTERS

THE SCIENCE OF
HURRICANES

Joanne Mattern

Cavendish Square

Published in 2020 by Cavendish Square Publishing, LLC
243 5th Avenue, Suite 136, New York, NY 10016

Copyright © 2020 by Cavendish Square Publishing, LLC

First Edition

Website: cavendishsq.com

This publication represents the opinions and views of the author based on his or her personal experience, knowledge, and research. The information in this book serves as a general guide only. The author and publisher have used their best efforts in preparing this book and disclaim liability rising directly or indirectly from the use and application of this book.

All websites were available and accurate when this book was sent to press.

Library of Congress Cataloging-in-Publication Data

Names: Mattern, Joanne, 1963- author.
Title: The science of hurricanes / Joanne Mattern.
Description: First edition. | New York : Cavendish Square, 2020. |
Series: The science of natural disasters | Audience: Grades 2 to 5. | Includes bibliographical references and index.
Identifiers: LCCN 2018060542 (print) | LCCN 2019000505 (ebook) |
ISBN 9781502646538 (ebook) | ISBN 9781502646521 (library bound) | ISBN 9781502646507 (pbk.) |
ISBN 9781502646514 (6 pack) Subjects: LCSH: Hurricanes--Juvenile literature. |
Hurricane protection--Juvenile literature.Classification: LCC QC944.2 (ebook) |
LCC QC944.2 .M3755 2020 (print) | DDC 551.55/2--dc23LC record available at https://lccn.loc.gov/2018060542

Editorial Director: David McNamara
Editor: Kristen Susienka
Copy Editor: Nathan Heidelberger
Associate Art Director: Alan Sliwinski
Designer: Ginny Kemmerer
Production Coordinator: Karol Szymczuk
Photo Research: J8 Media

Printed in the United States of America

CONTENTS

People struggle to walk through the storm as Hurricane Dean strikes Mexico in 2007.

CHAPTER 1

WHAT IS A HURRICANE LIKE?

In the middle of September 2018, people living along the East Coast of the United States got some very bad news. A huge hurricane named Florence was headed their way. People got ready for the storm. They prepared for high winds, heavy rain, and floods. Many people evacuated, or left the area. Others boarded up their windows and prepared for the danger.

What Is a Hurricane?

A hurricane is a big storm. It forms over warm ocean waters. It gathers **energy** from the warm waters.

If you see a photo of a hurricane, you will notice thick clouds gathered around a hole. That hole is called the eye. The eye is a calm part of the storm, but it means the storm is still happening. The clouds around the eye are called wall clouds. Winds swirl around the eye. The wall clouds fill with rain.

Hurricanes can be seen from space. This picture of Hurricane Florence was taken from the International Space Station in 2018.

DID YOU KNOW?

A hurricane's official name is a tropical cyclone. However, hurricanes have different names in other parts of the world. In Southeast Asia, they are called typhoons. In central Asia, they are called cyclones.

Many hurricanes stay in the ocean. Others go toward land. If a hurricane reaches land, it can cause lots of damage. Winds over 70 miles per hour (113 kilometers per hour) knock down trees and power lines. These high winds can blow roofs off

A man fights against a crashing wave during a typhoon in the Philippines in 2012.

Waves rush ashore as Hurricane Rita washes over Lake Charles, Louisiana, in 2005.

houses and knock down buildings.

Hurricanes also bring heavy rain. Hurricane Harvey struck Texas in 2017. The storm moved slowly over land. Rain fell for many hours. Some places got more than 4 feet (1.2 meters) of rain. Streets flooded. Thousands of homes and businesses filled with water. More than eighty people died.

Inside the Storm

Hurricanes can include many different dangers. One of the most dangerous and dramatic is called a storm surge. A storm surge forms when the low **air pressure** inside a hurricane pulls in warm, wet ocean air. The pressure can also pull water onto land in a big rush.

Hurricane Sandy's storm surge was so powerful it washed this roller coaster out to sea in Seaside Heights, New Jersey.

UNDERSTANDING HURRICANES

Areas of tropical hurricane formation

Typical paths of hurricanes

This map shows where in North America the most hurricanes happen and their paths.

Hurricanes begin in tropical ocean waters. These areas are found in the southern part of the Atlantic Ocean and in the southern Pacific and Indian Oceans. Atlantic storms usually form between the western coast of Africa and the Caribbean Sea.

These storms may strike the Caribbean islands, Central America, and the southern part of the United States. Or they may move up the East Coast of the United States. Once in a while, they will head east and strike the coast of England. Hurricanes in the Pacific and Indian Oceans affect Australia and many countries in Asia.

During Hurricane Sandy, storm surges caused flooding many miles from the ocean shore.

High winds and low pressure inside a hurricane can create thunderstorms. Sometimes these thunderstorms form tornadoes or **waterspouts**.

A waterspout hovers near the harbor in Singapore.

Strong waves churn warm ocean waters that fuel hurricanes.

CHAPTER 2

THE HOW AND WHY OF HURRICANES

Hurricanes form when areas of low pressure and high pressure meet. Warm air and cold air **masses** come together to make a powerful storm.

Highs and Lows

The part of Earth near the **equator** is called the tropics. This area is hot. The coldest places on Earth are the North and South Poles. Earth's atmosphere and its

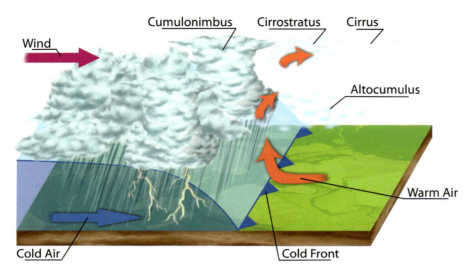

Wind Cumulonimbus Cirrostratus Cirrus

Altocumulus

Warm Air

Cold Air Cold Front

This diagram shows how a cold front pulls up warm air and causes air masses to move.

oceans are always moving hot and cold air masses and water around. Hot air masses move from the tropics toward the poles. Warm ocean **currents** also move this way. Cold air masses and cold ocean currents move from the poles to the equator.

Hot and cold air masses often meet in the tropics. These masses have different air pressures. When hot and cold masses meet over a warm ocean, a current of warm, wet air rises to meet the cooler air above it. As the warm air rises, cold air rushes in to fill the space. This creates a strong wind. At the same time, Earth's rotation causes the winds to spin around. If the winds spin fast enough, they create a tropical storm.

Tropical Storm or Hurricane?

A weather system becomes a tropical storm when its winds reach 39 miles per hour (63 kmh). If the wind

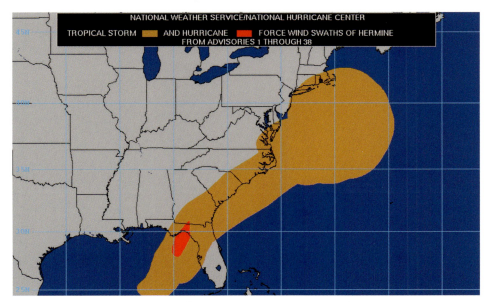

NATIONAL WEATHER SERVICE/NATIONAL HURRICANE CENTER

TROPICAL STORM   AND HURRICANE   FORCE WIND SWATHS OF HERMINE
FROM ADVISORIES 1 THROUGH 38

This map shows the path of Hurricane Hermine up the East Coast in 2016.

speed reaches 74 miles per hour (119 kmh), the storm is called a hurricane. Tropical storms are bad, but hurricanes are worse.

The Path of the Storm

Hurricanes form over warm oceans. They do not stay in one place. The wind moves them across the water. A hurricane can move about 10 to 20 miles per hour (16 to 32 kmh).

As hurricanes move over oceans, they gain strength from the warm water below. However, when a hurricane gets to land, it doesn't have warm

The forces of hurricane waves and wind completely destroyed this beach house.

This image shows waves hitting a town in New England in 1938. The waves were part of a hurricane.

water to give it power. A hurricane usually becomes weaker as it travels over land. The storm's winds die down. The hurricane might turn back into a tropical storm. As the storm loses more power, the winds and rain finally end.

Predicting a Storm

Meteorologists study weather patterns. They help predict different storms. These scientists watch where the storms go. They also tell people what the path of the storm will be and what damage it could cause.

Before the 1950s, there were few ways to know if a hurricane was coming. People didn't know about a storm until it was too late. They did not have a chance to protect themselves or get out of harm's way. Today, we have many ways to find out when and where a hurricane will strike.

During the 1950s and 1960s, meteorologists began to use **satellites** to track storms. Satellites helped them see storms form and move. Computers also helped scientists figure out which way a storm was moving.

DID YOU KNOW?

Hurricanes have had names since 1953. If a storm is very serious, its name will not be used again.

Then meteorologists could warn people that a hurricane was heading in their direction. This gave people time to prepare for the storm or leave the area. These warnings saved many lives.

Tech Tools

Today, scientists use radar to track storms. Radar sends a radio signal into the air. The signal bounces off any objects in its path. Meteorologists use radar to see how

This satellite image shows the position of Hurricane Florence over the Atlantic Ocean and the United States in 2018.

big a hurricane is. Satellites send pictures back from space. These pictures show how big a hurricane is and where it is going.

One interesting but dangerous way to watch a hurricane is to fly inside it! Expert pilots fly special planes filled with equipment. They fly into the storm. There, they collect information on the temperature, wind speed, pressure, and rainfall inside the storm. This information helps scientists on the ground learn more about the storm. The more meteorologists know about hurricanes, the more prepared people can be when a bad storm strikes.

DID YOU KNOW?

The average life of a hurricane is nine days. The longest storm ever recorded was Typhoon John. It struck the Pacific Ocean in 1994. That storm lasted thirty-one days, from August to September.

THE SAFFIR-SIMPSON HURRICANE WIND SCALE

In 1971, two scientists developed the Saffir-Simpson Hurricane Wind Scale. This scale measures wind strength in a hurricane on a scale from 1 to 5. Each number is called a category. A category 1 hurricane has dangerous winds that will cause some damage. A category 5 hurricane has winds so strong that almost everything will be destroyed. This scale is still used today.

Saffir/Simpson Hurricane Scale

Category	Definition
1	Winds 75–95 mph (120–153 kmh)
2	Winds 96–110 mph (154–177 kmh)
3	Winds 111–130 mph (179–209 kmh)
4	Winds 131–155 mph (211–249 kmh)
5	Winds greater than 155 mph (249 kmh+)

Men work to board up windows of a home before Hurricane Irma strikes in 2017.

CHAPTER 3

PREPARING FOR AND PREDICTING A HURRICANE

Today, meteorologists give people important information when a hurricane is on the way. It is important to listen to meteorologists and take action if a hurricane is heading toward you.

How to Prepare for a Hurricane

If you have to evacuate, you and your family should make a plan before the storm strikes. Map out several ways to leave your town. Decide on where you will stay once you leave.

If you stay home, make sure you have an emergency kit ready. Put food, water, batteries, flashlights, a battery-powered radio, medical supplies, a cell phone, and basic tools in it.

It is also important to protect your home. Some

Families should make an evacuation plan before a storm strikes.

homes have hurricane shutters. These heavy wooden boards cover the windows and keep them from breaking. Other people put plywood over their windows before a storm. Make sure your family protects your house.

Downed tree limbs and power lines create deadly danger.

Bring in any outside objects that might fly away during a storm. Items such as garbage cans, grills, and yard decorations can become very dangerous if the wind picks them up.

After the Storm

After the storm is over, danger still remains. Live power lines are down. Trees block roads. Rushing water washes away streets and bridges. It can take days or even weeks for neighborhoods to get power again. Cell phone service may be affected too.

Are Hurricanes Getting Worse?

Today, many people believe that hurricanes are getting stronger. They also seem to be happening more often. One reason for this is **climate change**.

Hurricanes are part of a normal pattern of weather. Some years there are a lot of hurricanes. Other years there are just a few. However, many scientists believe

DID YOU KNOW?

Meteorologists used to look at past hurricanes to see what new hurricanes might do. Today, they use supercomputers to create prediction models that show where a storm will hit.

Scientists study a computer model of Hurricane Gustav in 2008.

that climate change is creating more powerful hurricanes. They point out that Earth's temperature is getting warmer. Ocean temperatures are rising. This could mean that hurricanes are more likely to form. Rising sea levels also mean that flooding is worse.

No one can know exactly when a hurricane will happen or how it will behave. The best we can do is study storms and be prepared when the next hurricane arrives.

RIDING OUT THE STORM

When a bad hurricane is predicted, the government often tells people to evacuate. However, many people stay behind. Why? Sometimes people do not have a place to go. They may not have a car or another way to travel out of the area. Other people decide to stay because they cannot bring their pets. It might be difficult for the elderly, the disabled, or very young children to travel. Sometimes,

A man walks alone through a neighborhood damaged by Hurricane Katrina in 2005.

people want to stay home to protect their property. Still more don't believe the hurricane will be that bad, or they have stayed for other storms in the past and believe they can get through the next one too.

GLOSSARY

air pressure The force that presses down from the weight of the air.

climate change A change in climate patterns around the world, caused by humans.

currents Water or air moving in one direction.

energy Something that gives things power.

equator An invisible line running around the middle of Earth.

masses Large bodies of matter.

satellites Metal objects that fly around Earth and record information.

waterspouts Spinning columns of water.

FIND OUT MORE

Books

Rivera, Andrea. *Hurricanes*. Minneapolis, MN: Abdo Zoom, 2018.

Shofner, Melissa. *Hammered by Hurricanes*. Natural Disasters: How People Survive. New York: PowerKids Press, 2018.

Website

10 Facts About Hurricanes!

https://www.natgeokids.com/au/discover/geography/physical-geography/hurricanes

Learn some interesting facts about hurricanes at this information-packed site.

Video

Hurricane Facts for Kids

https://www.youtube.com/watch?v=2kLwbb0ggFU

Watch this video to learn about hurricanes, what creates them, and the damage they cause.

INDEX

Page numbers in **boldface** refer to images. Entries in **boldface** are glossary terms.

ABOUT THE AUTHOR

Joanne Mattern is the author of hundreds of nonfiction books for children. Storms are one of her favorite subjects to write about, along with sports, history, animals, and biography. Mattern lives in New York State with her husband, children, and an assortment of pets. She has experienced a few hurricanes in her life.